Blastoff! Readers are carefully developed by literacy experts to build reading stamina and move students toward fluency by combining standards-based content with developmentally appropriate text.

 Level 1 provides the most support through repetition of high-frequency words, light text, predictable sentence patterns, and strong visual support.

 Level 2 offers early readers a bit more challenge through varied sentences, increased text load, and text-supportive special features.

 Level 3 advances early-fluent readers toward fluency through increased text load, less reliance on photos, advancing concepts, longer sentences, and more complex special features.

★ **Blastoff! Universe**

This edition first published in 2024 by Bellwether Media, Inc.

No part of this publication may be reproduced in whole or in part without written permission of the publisher. For information regarding permission, write to Bellwether Media, Inc., Attention: Permissions Department, 6012 Blue Circle Drive, Minnetonka, MN 55343.

Library of Congress Cataloging-in-Publication Data

LC record for Mountain Lions available at: https://lccn.loc.gov/2023046596

Text copyright © 2024 by Bellwether Media, Inc. BLASTOFF! READERS and associated logos are trademarks and/or registered trademarks of Bellwether Media, Inc.

Editor: Betsy Rathburn   Designer: Brittany McIntosh

Printed in the United States of America, North Mankato, MN.

Table of Contents

One Cat, Many Names	4
Leaping Mountain Lions	8
Hide and Seek	12
Starting Out Spotted	18
Glossary	22
To Learn More	23
Index	24

One Cat, Many Names

Mountain lions are wild cats known by many names. People also call them pumas, cougars, or panthers.

Mountain lions live in forests, deserts, mountains, and **wetlands**.

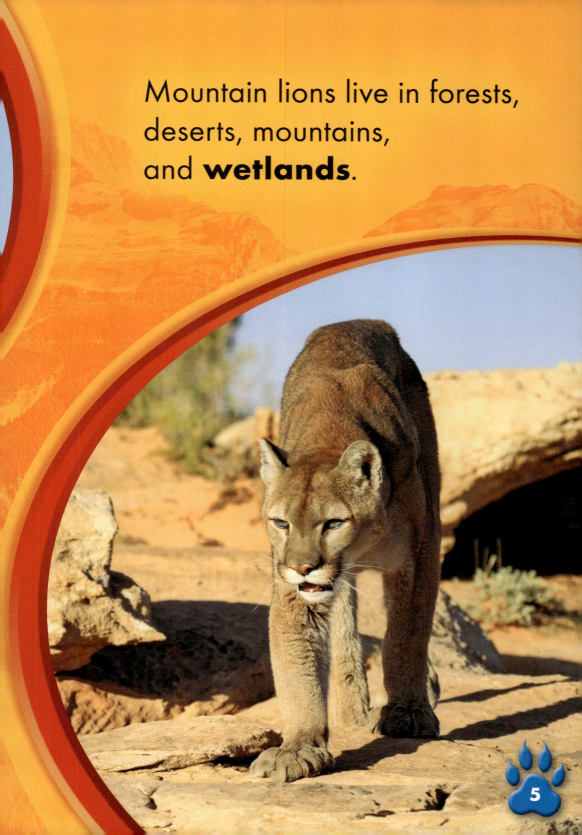

Mountain lions have a huge range. They can be found across North and South America.

Mountain lions are plentiful across their range. But their numbers are dropping. **Habitat** loss harms these animals. People also hunt them.

Leaping Mountain Lions

Mountain lions have tan or gray fur. They have darker fur on their ears and tails.

Their back legs are longer than their front legs. This lets them leap over 40 feet (12 meters) in one jump!

Identify a Mountain Lion

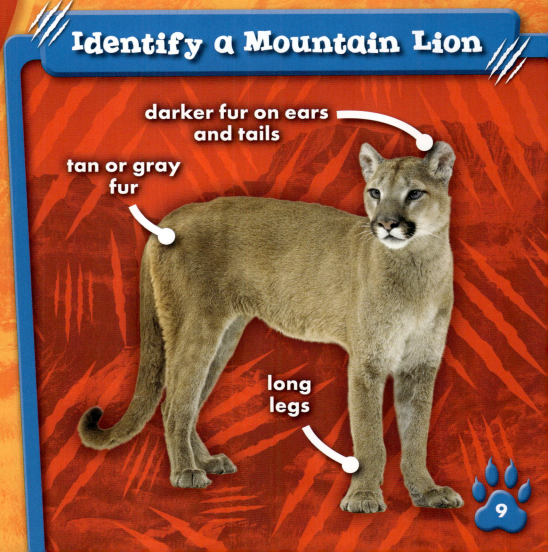

- darker fur on ears and tails
- tan or gray fur
- long legs

Mountain lions can grow to be around 5 feet (1.5 meters) long. Their tails add 3 feet (0.9 meters) to their length!

Size Comparison

house cat

height at shoulder
around 10 inches
(25 centimeters)

length (without tail)
around 18 inches
(46 centimeters)

mountain lion

height at shoulder
around 30 inches
(76 centimeters)

length (without tail)
around 60 inches
(152 centimeters)

Females weigh up to 130 pounds (59 kilograms). Males can weigh over 180 pounds (82 kilograms).

Hide and Seek

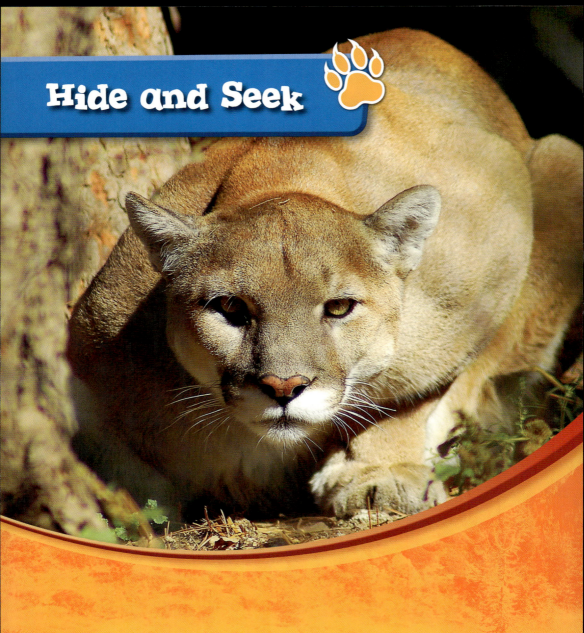

Mountain lions often hunt in the morning and evening. Great eyesight helps them find **prey**.

These cats are mainly **ambush** hunters. They sneak up on prey. Then, they attack!

Mountain lions are **carnivores**. They often eat deer. They also hunt rabbits, raccoons, and marmots.

Mountain lions store their food in **caches**. They come back later to eat it.

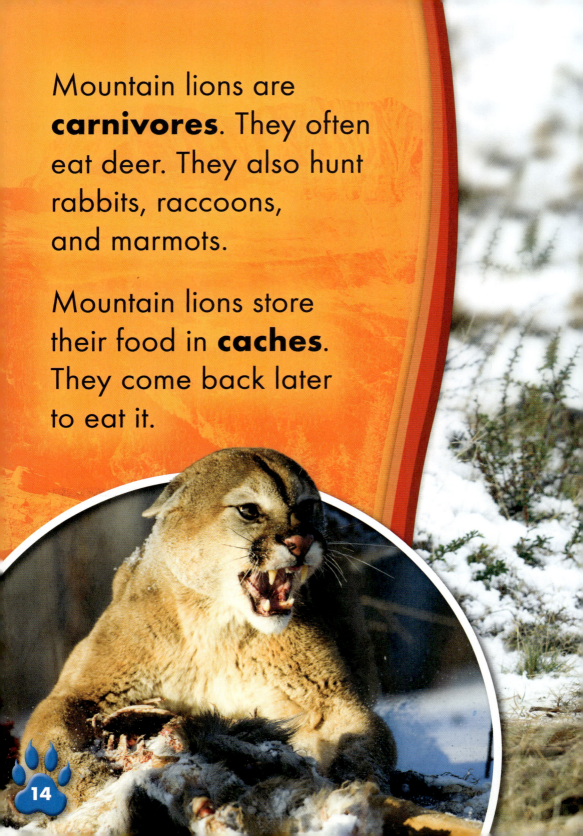

These animals are **solitary**. Females may travel with their babies. But mountain lions mostly live alone.

They mark their **territory** to keep other mountain lions away. They scratch trees and leave claw marks in dirt.

Starting Out Spotted

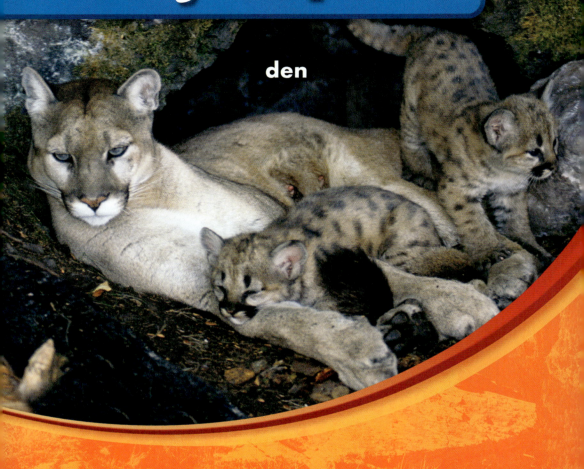

den

Female mountain lions have **litters** of up to six cubs. The babies stay in a **den** for around six weeks.

Newborn cubs have spotted fur. The spots disappear within nine months.

Baby Mountain Lions

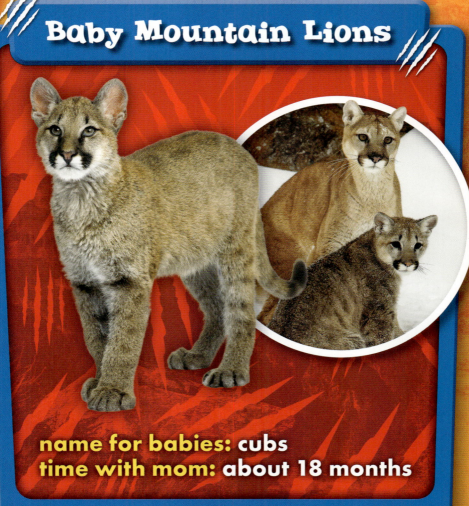

name for babies: cubs
time with mom: about 18 months

Mountain lion cubs follow their mom when she hunts. She teaches them how to catch prey.

Cubs stay with their mom for around 18 months. After that, they are on their own!

In the Wild

habitats:

forests   deserts   mountains   wetlands

conservation status: least concern

| Least Concern | Near Threatened | Vulnerable | Endangered | Critically Endangered | Extinct in the Wild | Extinct |

population in the wild: less than 50,000
population trend: going down
life span: up to 20 years

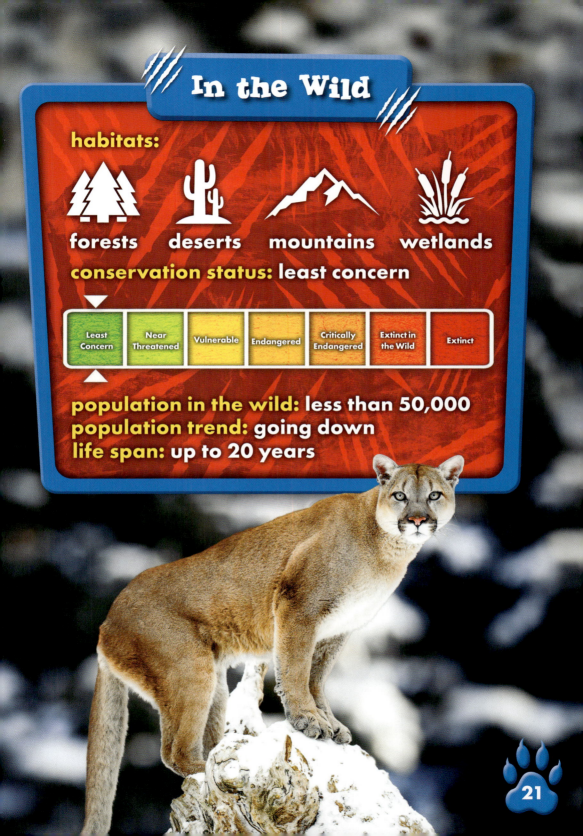

Glossary

ambush—an attack from a hiding place

caches—hidden places used to store food

carnivores—animals that only eat meat

den—a sheltered place

habitat—a land area with certain types of plants, animals, and weather

litters—groups of babies that are born at the same time

prey—animals that are hunted by other animals for food

solitary—living alone

territory—the land area where an animal lives

wetlands—areas of land that are covered with low levels of water for most of the year

To Learn More

AT THE LIBRARY
Humphrey, Natalie. *Leopard Seal vs. Cougar*. New York, N.Y.: Gareth Stevens Publishing, 2023.

Sanderson, Whitney. *Meet a Baby Mountain Lion*. Minneapolis, Minn.: Lerner Publications, 2024.

Shaffer, Lindsay. *Mountain Lions*. Minneapolis, Minn.: Bellwether Media, 2020.

ON THE WEB

FACTSURFER

Factsurfer.com gives you a safe, fun way to find more information.

1. Go to www.factsurfer.com.

2. Enter "mountain lions" into the search box and click 🔍.

3. Select your book cover to see a list of related content.

Index

ambush hunters, 13
caches, 14
carnivores, 14
claw marks, 17
colors, 8
cubs, 16, 18, 19, 20
den, 18
deserts, 5
ears, 8
eyesight, 12
females, 11, 16, 18, 20
food, 14, 15
forests, 5
fur, 8, 19
habitat loss, 7
hunt, 7, 12, 13, 14, 20
identify, 9
in the wild, 21
jump, 9
legs, 9
litters, 18
males, 11
mountains, 5
names, 4

North America, 6
numbers, 7
prey, 12, 13, 14, 15, 20
range, 6, 7
scratch, 17
size, 10, 11
size comparison, 11
solitary, 16
South America, 6
spots, 19
tails, 8, 10
territory, 17
wetlands, 5

The images in this book are reproduced through the courtesy of: Eric Isselee, front cover (mountain lion), pp. 3, 19 (cub), 22; Peter Stein, front cover (background); Scenic Shutterbug, p. 4; imageBROKER.com GmbH & Co. KG/ Alamy, p. 5; Jim Cumming, pp. 6, 10-11; Dennis W Donohue, p. 8; Ultrashock, p. 9; Nynke van Holten, p. 11 (house cat); Anan Kaewkhammul, p. 11 (mountain lion); joesephfotos, p. 12; David Bates, p. 13; jimkruger, p. 14; Octavio Campos Salles/ Alamy, pp. 14-15; Tracy Hart, p. 15 (deer); Griffin Gillespie, p. 15 (raccoons); Wirestock Creators, p. 15 (marmots); Scott E Read, p. 16; outdoorsman, p. 17; Ken Cole/ Age Fotostock, p. 18; Danita Delimont, pp. 19 (inset), 20; Evgeniyqw, pp. 20-21.